Making It Go

The Life and Work of Robert Fulton

Don Herweck

Physical Science Readers: Making It Go: The Life and Work of Robert Fulton

Publishing Credits

Editorial Director
Dona Herweck Rice

Associate Editor
Joshua BishopRoby

Editor-in-Chief
Sharon Coan, M.S.Ed.

Creative Director
Lee Aucoin

Illustration Manager
Timothy J. Bradley

Publisher
Rachelle Cracchiolo, M.S.Ed.

Science Contributor
Sally Ride Science

Science Consultants
Michael E. Kopecky,
Science Department Chair,
Chino Hills High School
Jane Weir, MPhys

Teacher Created Materials
5301 Oceanus Drive
Huntington Beach, CA 92649-1030
http://www.tcmpub.com

ISBN 978-0-7439-0578-7

Table of Contents

Always an Inventor

Robert Fulton is best known for creating the first successful **steamboat**. That is really just a small part of what he did. He was an inventor, artist, statesman, **mechanic**, and **engineer**. From the beginning, he spent his days learning and trying new things.

Fulton was born in Pennsylvania in 1765. His father died when he was just three. His mother was left to raise him and his siblings alone. When Fulton was just eight, his mother sent him away to school. But she became worried. She didn't think he was learning enough there.

She told his teacher of her concerns. The teacher said there wasn't much he could do. He thought that Fulton's "head was so full of original ideas that there was no room for . . . the contents of dusty books." Fulton didn't want to learn about what others said and did. He wanted to figure things out for himself.

Laws of Motion

Every engineer must learn the **Laws of Motion**. Sir Isaac Newton first came up with them about 300 years ago. They explain the effects of **force** on motion. The first law says that an object at rest will stay at rest if there is no outside force to put it into motion. It also says that a moving object will keep going in a straight line at the same speed forever unless there are outside forces. The second law says that a force makes an object speed up or slow down. The third law says that if a force is used, something happens in response to it that equals its power.

Force is needed to make planes take off, fly, and land.

Fulton began to invent things when he was a young boy. When he was 13 years old, he made his own pencils. He used sheets of lead. Pencils were not new at that time. But Robert's pencils were just as good as the **graphite** pencils that were invented before this time.

Fulton was very smart, but he never did well in school. He learned how to read and write at home. He did not like to do his schoolwork. He wanted to work at the mechanics shop instead.

Gunmaker

Fulton was an expert gunmaker, too. When he was a teen, he made parts for gun makers.

As a boy, Fulton made his own pencils.

Early Engineers

Engineering has been around for a long time. It is the use of science and math to design, build, and operate buildings, machines, and systems. Heron of Alexandria was one of the first engineers. The exact date of his birth is unknown. But some experts believe he was born around A.D. 75. He is worth noting because he made a steam engine that helped a great deal in developing the first jet engine.

In addition to working in mechanics, Robert was an artist. In fact, as a young man, his dream was to become a painter. In 1786, he went to London to study art. Making a living as an artist was difficult. So, he returned to his engineering work. He used his artisitic skills to sketch his inventions.

An important thing to note about Fulton is that he did more than just think of new inventions. He also designed and built most of his ideas.

Fulton was quite the artist. This is one of his sketches, *Cruelty Presiding over the Prison Ship*, done in 1856.

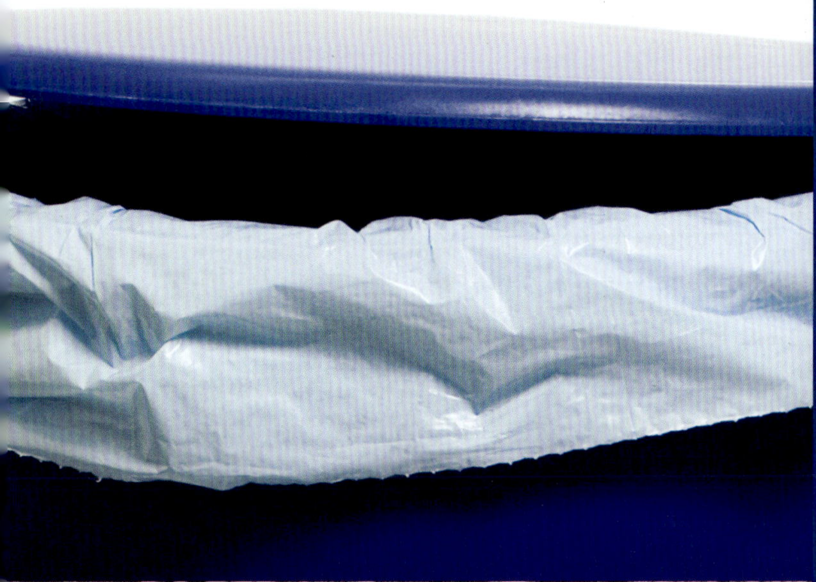

Lillian Gilbreth

Lillian Gilbreth was born in 1878. She earned degrees in literature, but she became famous for other things. First, she had twelve children. One of them wrote the famous novel **Cheaper by the Dozen** about their family. The second is that she became an important engineer. During the Great Depression, Gilbreth helped the president of the United States find ways to make work more efficient. She also invented many things you use every day. These include the foot-pedal trashcan and refrigerator door shelves. Gilbreth was also the first woman elected to the National Academy of Engineering. She lived to be 94 years old.

Working with Boats

Robert Fulton always liked boats. He spent much of his life looking for new ways to propel boats through the water. The fishing boats of his time moved by "poling." This was done by pushing a long pole against the bottom of a river. Robert wanted to make a better boat. He designed a boat with paddle wheels and a crank. The boat did not look very nice, but it worked well.

Here you can see the hand crank used to paddle the boat and the rudder used to steer it by.

Paving the Way

In 1918, Kate Gleason became the first female member of the American Society of Mechanical Engineers.

Martha J. Coston

They say that necessity is the mother of invention. They also say that you can do anything you set your mind to. Martha J. Coston proves that both are true. When she was just 21, her husband died. She was left to care for their four children alone. It was the mid-1800s. Coston didn't have many options. She found plans for a **signal flare** in her husband's notes. She took his idea and made it better. Coston used the **technology** of fireworks to help make bright, safe, long-lasting flares. The U.S. Navy gave her $20,000 for her invention. With that money, she started an engineering company. It lasted until the late 1970s.

Making Them Better

Robert Fulton often worked to improve earlier inventions. Most people think he invented the **steam engine**. The steam engine had actually been invented before Fulton's work. Fulton, however, was the first to put the design ideas into action. He studied the ways that steam could be used to move boats through the water. In 1807, Fulton built the *Clermont*. It was the first steamboat that could be called a success.

Measure Up!

Any good engineer knows that nothing can be done without good measurements. Fulton had to be exact when it came to building his steamboat. These are his measurements for the *Clermont*.

Length: 43 meters (142 feet)
Maximum height: 19 meters (62 feet)
Maximum width: 4.3 meters (14 feet)
Draught: 4.8 meters (15 feet 9 inches)
Displacement: 1,210 tons
Average Speed: 4.7 miles per hour
Distance Traveled: 150 miles in thirty-two hours

Early Steam Engine

Thomas Savery (1650–1716) built the first steam engine. It was used to pump water out of coal mines.

Canals

In 1796, Fulton wrote a paper about **canals**. Canals are waterways. Fulton thought small boats on canals would be better than carts and horses on roads for transporting goods and people. So, he designed new types of canal boats. He also thought of a way to drag boats up hills between canals. Water wheels and pulleys were used to do this.

British leaders liked Fulton's ideas. They needed canals to move coal from mines to the city. Fulton was hired to make the canals in England better.

This image shows a modern lock system at work.

Construction of the Panama Canal

Canal to the World

Canals help move heavy loads over water. The Panama Canal allows ships to move between two oceans. A French engineer started to build it in 1878. The United States finished it in 1914. In 1999, the United States gave Panama control of the canal. Today, the Panama Canal is used to shorten the routes of commercial ships. Also, cruise ships use it to move between the Atlantic and Pacific Oceans.

Panama Canal locks in 1913 before it opened to ship traffic in 1914

Robert Fulton continued his canal work for many years. One important invention that improved the use of canals was the double inclined plane. This could be used to raise and lower boats in and out of canals. An **inclined plane** is shaped like a wedge. It allows heavy loads to be raised with less energy. A load would be much harder to lift without it.

Fulton showed how one plane could be used to raise a boat. The other plane was used to lower a boat at the same time. Fulton's design used water as the energy source. It also used pulleys with chains to connect the two boats. This was a very useful invention!

Fulton's double inclined plane made it much easier to lower and lift boats into and out of the water.

Canal Clean Up

In 2005, Hurricane Katrina struck. It caused a lot of damage. Much of the damage was caused because the levee systems failed. Whole neighborhoods were flooded. That's when engineers like Karen Lahare stepped in. She managed a huge canal clearing project in the state of Louisiana. She and her team cleared more than 112 kilometers (70 miles) of canals.

Pyramid Planes

Inclined planes were used to build the pyramids in Egypt. Egyptians used inclined planes that were over a mile long.

Diving Boats

Fulton wondered about underwater travel. How could it be possible? He wanted to find a way. In 1800, he made a diving boat. It was made of wood and metal. Water put into tanks would add weight to it. This weight would push the boat down. When water was pushed out of the tanks, the boat floated up.

Fulton built a dome on top of the boat. The dome had thick windows to see through. The crew would get in the boat through the dome. A hand crank turned a propeller. This powered the diving boat underwater.

Does this kind of vehicle sound familiar? Fulton's diving boat is what we now call a **submarine**.

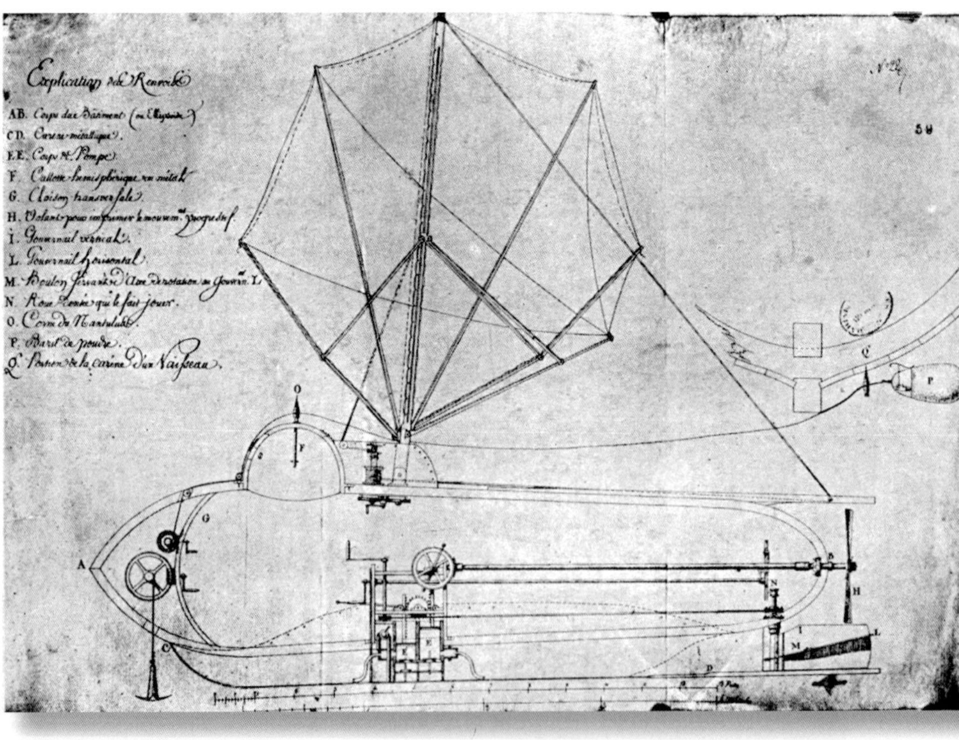

Fulton's diving boat

Modern submarines

Submarines

Submarines have changed a lot over time. In 1954, the first nuclear-powered submarine was made. It can stay under the water for a long time. Sailors can live for months below the sea in such a submarine. Modern submarines have changed **warfare**, too. Early submarines had to come to the surface to fire missiles. Submarines today can fire missiles under the water. Submarine missiles can travel long distances to their targets.

It was Napoleon, the great leader of France, who asked Fulton to design the first practical submarine. The model he built was called the *Nautilus*.

Fulton gave his diving boat design to French leaders in 1801. He planned the **hull** to be armored. That would protect it from cannonballs. The boat was designed to have a small crew of sailors. They would turn a crank to move the boat. The crew had to raise a mast and sail when above water. Fulton used a **compass** to direct the boat under the water.

Fulton led tests with a group of three men from the government to review his plans. Fulton and the others remained under water for three hours. They were able to raise and lower the boat by filling and emptying water from tanks. The boat could go to depths of nearly 8 meters (25 feet). The pressure of the water any deeper would have crushed the hull.

Naomi Leonard

Dr. Naomi Leonard is a modern engineer. She recently received a big award to continue her work: $500,000. The money is known as a "genius grant." It was given to her because she shows so much creative and original thinking in her work. She designs ways to control robot vehicles under the water. These vehicles are sent to patrol the seas. They can stay for long periods of time—much longer than a human can. While there, they gather data about sea life. The data they get can help to reveal what happens deep beneath the surface.

Maritime Warfare

Robert Fulton lived during a time of many wars. At that time, the British navy ruled the seas. Fulton wished for world peace. Yet, he combined many of his inventions to make weapons. Fulton hoped his weapons would end wars. He tried to sell his weapons to both the United States and countries in Europe. He thought in this way he could help to bring peace.

Fulton put underwater cannons onto boats. Before that time, cannonballs were shot onto decks of other ships. They put holes in the ships or damaged the sails. The ship would sink or slow down. Fulton's new cannons could shoot into the sides of ships. This would put holes in the ships under the water level. Water would then rush into the ships' hulls. This made the ships sink faster.

Fulton also made torpedoes with gunpowder that could explode underwater. He designed his diving boat to tow the torpedoes. His boat could tow a torpedo under a ship and then set the fuse. This would blow up the ship's hull and sink the ship.

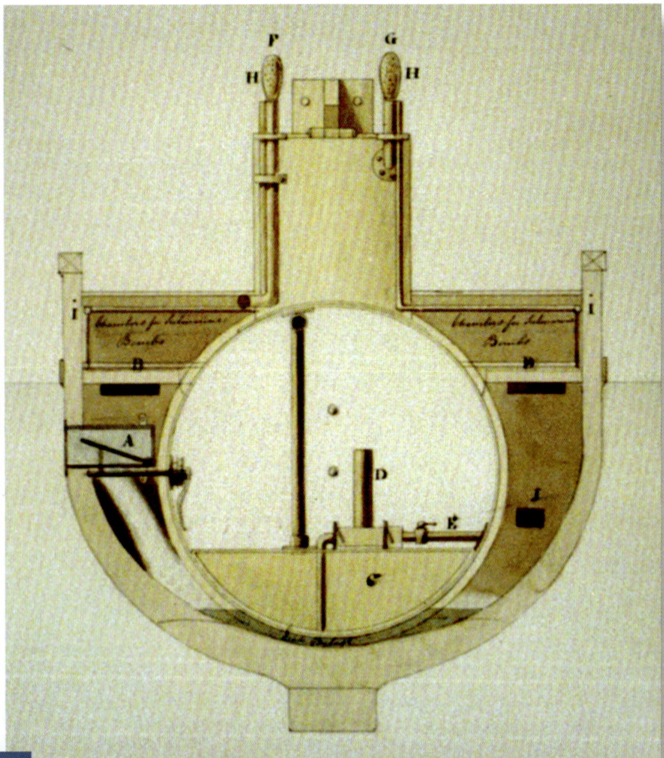

This sketch done by Fulton in 1806 shows a cross section through a "plunging boat."

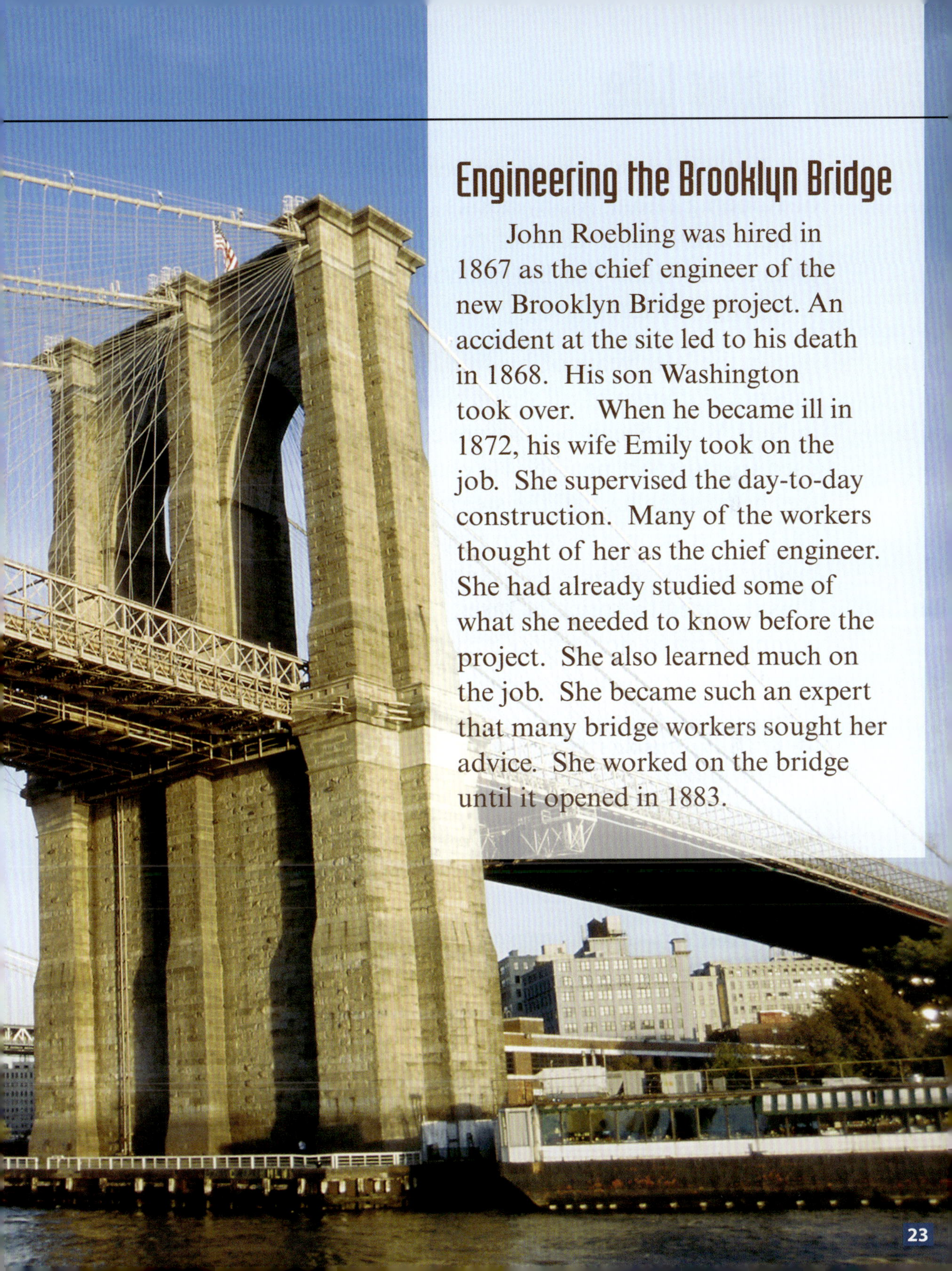

Engineering the Brooklyn Bridge

John Roebling was hired in 1867 as the chief engineer of the new Brooklyn Bridge project. An accident at the site led to his death in 1868. His son Washington took over. When he became ill in 1872, his wife Emily took on the job. She supervised the day-to-day construction. Many of the workers thought of her as the chief engineer. She had already studied some of what she needed to know before the project. She also learned much on the job. She became such an expert that many bridge workers sought her advice. She worked on the bridge until it opened in 1883.

Later Life

Little is known about the personal life of Robert Fulton. Many books have been written about him. Each of these mainly gives a long history of his inventions. A few things are known.

In the later years of his life, Fulton was put in charge of all steamboat traffic in New York. Steamboats were commonly used to transport people. He charged high fees because he had all the steamboats. In 1818, other people began to run steamboat businesses. Now there was competition. This dropped the price of fares. Fulton's company could not stay in business.

At one time, steamboats did the work that modern ferries do today.

Some of New York's waterways today

Fulton did not live a long life. He developed lung problems that started with a bad cold. He became very sick. In 1815, at the age of 49, he died in New York. It is said that his death "deprived the United States of one of her most useful citizens."

Robert Fulton spent his life as an inventor, mechanic, and engineer. His work lives on in his inventions. It also lives in the work of engineers that came after him. Even today, engineers use his work to develop ideas and inventions of their own.

Roboticist: Cynthia Breazeal

Sally Ride Science

Massachusetts Institute of Technology

Bot Buddies

Meet the woman who could make *Star Wars* real. "I saw *Star Wars* when I was really young," Cynthia Breazeal says. "I really adored R2-D2 and C-3PO. Having robots like that someday captivated my imagination."

Becoming an astronaut and going to Mars also captured her imagination. Breazeal started designing robots that might one day explore Mars.

Now she designs robots like the furry guy below named Leonardo. He's programmed to behave like a friend.

When Breazeal is not in the lab, you can find her surfing or snowboarding. "When I was growing up, I was probably known much more as an athlete than as a scholar." Maybe someday she'll design a bot to join her on the slopes.

Robots like Breazeal designs can be used for both work and play.

Is It 4 U?

If you were a roboticist, you might . . .

- design machines that build cars.
- build hi-tech toys.
- program robots to explore Mars.

4 U 2 Do

Do you think you'll ever play sports against a robot? Draw a picture of what a robotic athlete might look like.

Lab: Pressure, That Sinking Feeling!

Mechanical engineers must know all about the way things work in order to design, build, and run them. For example, a submarine engineer must figure out how to make a boat submerge or float. Without this information, the submarine will be useless.

Try this lab to learn something about floating and submerging. You will be on your way to becoming a mechanical engineer!

Materials

- a clear plastic bottle with a tight lid, such as a water bottle
- a squeeze condiment packet, such as for ketchup
- a glass
- water

Procedure

1. Fill a glass with water.
2. Place your unopened condiment pack into the water. The packet should just barely float. If it sinks, try another type of packet.
3. After you have a good packet, fill a clear plastic bottle with water.

4 Put your unopened condiment packet into the bottle.

5 Screw the top on the bottle.

6 The condiment packet is now a "boat." Squeeze the bottle to make your boat submerge, or go downward.

7 To make your boat rise, simply relax your hand.

4

5

What Is Happening?

The bottle filled with water has pressure in it. The condiment packet has a small pocket of air in it. When the bottle is squeezed, the air pocket in the condiment packet is made smaller. This is similar to adding water to the ballast tank of the diving boat or submarine. The increased pressure pushes the boat downward. The decrease in pressure brings it back up.

6

7

Glossary

canal—a long channel of water artificially made for boats to travel along

compass—a device for finding direction using a freely moving needle that always points to magnetic north

engineer—to plan, build, or manage a building or construction project

graphite—a soft shiny black carbon that is used in making lead pencils

hull—the body or frame of a ship, most of which goes under the water

inclined plane—a simple machine for elevating objects

Laws of Motion—Sir Isaac Newton's three basic laws that describe the affects of force on motion

mechanic—someone whose job is repairing the engines of vehicles and other machines

signal flare—a very bright light or colored smoke which can be used as a signal, or a device which produces this

steamboat—a boat which moves by steam power

steam engine—an engine that converts the heat energy of pressurized steam into mechanical energy

submarine—a ship which can travel under water

technology—the application of science, especially to industrial or commercial objectives

warfare—military fighting between enemies

Index

Sally Ride Science

Sally Ride Science™ is an innovative content company dedicated to fueling young people's interests in science. Our publications and programs provide opportunities for students and teachers to explore the captivating world of science—from astrobiology to zoology. We bring science to life and show young people that science is creative, collaborative, fascinating, and fun.

Image Credits

Cover Getty Images; p.3 Photos.com; p.4 (top) Library of Congress; p.4 (bottom) The Granger Collection, New York; p.5 Photos.com; p.6-7 The Granger Collection, New York; p.7 (left) Johanna Goodyear/Shutterstock; p.7 (right) Costin Cojocaru/Shutterstock; p.8 (top) Public Domain; p.8 (bottom) The Granger Collection, New York; p.9 (back) Diego Cervo/Shutterstock; p.9 (front) The Granger Collection, New York; p.10 (top) Photos.com; p.10 (right) Tim Bradley; p.10 (left) Scott Laumann; p.11 (top) Scott Laumann; p.11 (bottom) Leo/Shutterstock; p. 12 (top) Tim Bradley; p.12 (bottom) Library of Congress; p.13 (left) Tim Bradley; p.13 (right) Mary Evans Picture Library/Alamy; p.14 (top) Israel Pabon/Shutterstockp; p.14 (bottom) Photos.com; p.15 (top) Library of Congress; p.15 (bottom) Library of Congress; p.16 (top) The Granger Collection, New York; p.16 (bottom) Library of Congress; p.17 (bottom) The Granger Collection, New York; p.18 (top) Library of Congress; p.18 (bottom) The Granger Collection, New York; p.19 (top) Harald Høiland Tjøstheim/Shutterstock; p.19 (left) Danilo ducak/Shutterstock; p.19 (right) Library of Congress; p.20 (top) Photos.com; p20 (bottom) Bettmann/Corbis; P. 21 (front) courtesy of Naomi Leonard; p.21 (back) Alexis Rosenfeld/Photo Researchers, Inc.; p.22 (top) Library of Congress; p.22 (bottom) Library of Congress; p.23 Photos.com; p.24 (top) Carsten Medom Madsen/Shutterstock; p.24 (bottom) Library of Congress; p.24–25 Photos.com; p.26 Sam Ogden/Photo Researchers, Inc.; p.27 Jason Grow; p28 Danilo ducak/Shutterstock; p.28–29 Nicoll Rager Fuller; p.32 Getty Images